Tassos Katsikas

# The Brandenburg-class Battleships 1890–1918

KAGERO

# Brandenburg class ship after the 1910 modernisation.

Starboard side view.

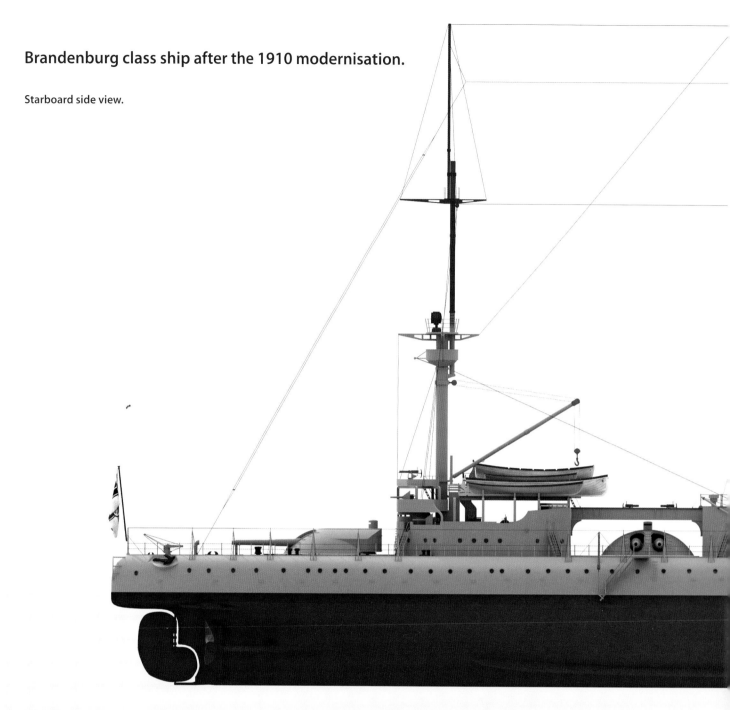

## Overview & Design

The *Brandenburg* class battleships were the first blue water warships of the *Kaiserliche Marine* (Imperial German Navy), in the end of 19th century, and can be categorized as the first German pre-dreadnought ships. Imperial German Navy was founded in 1871 under the auspices of *Kaiser Wilhem I*. The German Navy was created around the small Prussian Navy. Initially the Germans ordered several obsolete ironclads. However, the new German Navy was only capable for coastal defense operations and could not be considered as an instrument for the *WeltPolitik* and for the projection of German power worldwide. In 1888 the most modern ships of the German fleet were the six *Siegfried* class (3.400 tons) and two *Odin* class coastal defense ships. The new *Kaiser Wilhem II* the architect of the German Naval expansion, decided to challenge England's hegemony in the seas. As first step he established in 1888 the Imperial Naval Office (*Reichmarineamt*) a governmental agency monitoring the design, development and financing of the new fleet units. Under the leadership of Vice-Admiral *Alexander von Monts,* the Imperial Naval Office started to implement the naval visions of *Kaiser Wilhem II.*

    The ships of the *Brandenburg* class were the first tangible outcome of the new policy triggering a naval arms race between Germany and England. With 115.7 m length, 19.5m beam and displacement of 10013 tons, the Brandenburg class ships were the first wave of modern era battleships for *Kaiserliche Marine*, comparable to the British Royal *Sovereign* class ships, although the last ones new were at least 50% bigger than *Brandenburgs*. In the end of 19th century naval architecture was considered more as art and less as science. This was the main reason behind the adaptation of radical design approaches by many navies. The French and partially the Russian design bureaus adopted tumblehome hull design presenting strange looking ships like *Massena, Carnot, Iena,* and the Russian *Borodino.* Italians on the other hand were experimenting with groundbreaking guns distribution in a battleship (*Italia* class battleship). *Italia* was armed with a main battery of four 17" guns mounted in two pairs and arranged diagonally in a central barbette. So, in 1888 the German design bureaus decided to approach the design of the new ships from scratch. Instead of adopting the formal armament design with a couple of twin turrets in bow and stern and with many smaller guns, they proposed a new solution. As the ship was designed for open seas, they focused on a ship capable for engagement with enemy ships on longer ranges. Therefore, they suggested a combination of three turrets with 11" (28cm) guns for fight against large ships and several secondary smaller guns for fights against destroyers and torpedo boats. However, the bow and stern turrets carried 11" guns with 40L caliber, while the center turret carried 11"

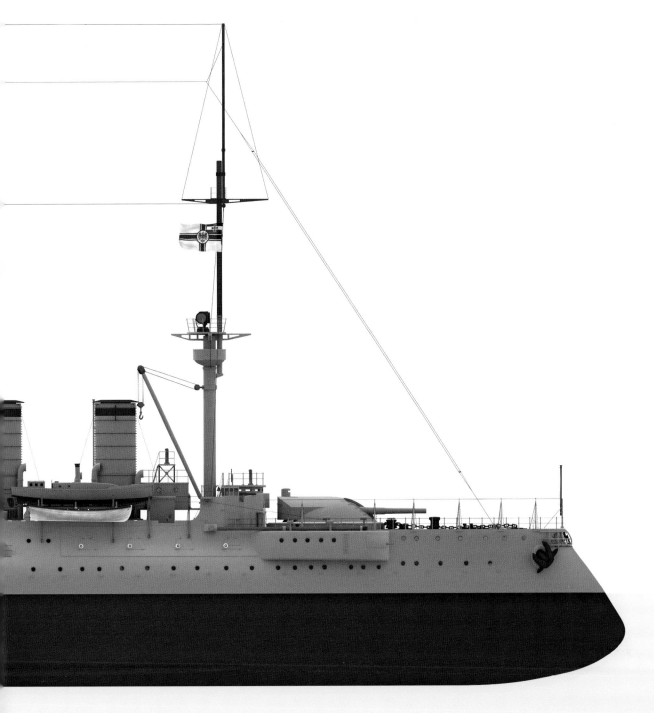

guns with 35L caliber because of the ship's superstructure. The three turrets approach was theoretically increasing by 50% the firepower of the main ship guns but had also some limitations. The disadvantage of this approach were the design compromises, as the center turret was occupying crucial space (normally used by coal and machinery), while more armor was required for the protection of the turret and the barbette. Because the center turret was mounted too low in the ship, causing blast damages to the surrounding decks. Because of the spatial (superstructure) limitations of the center turret, the 11"/35L guns could be loaded only when they were in a horizontal position. This was affecting the rate of fire (1 shell every 2 minutes). The Germans also adopted the (French origin) thick military masts for the Brandenburgs. The hull of the ship was constructed from transverse and longitudinal steel frames,

something later common for all the German warships. Brandenburgs also were the first German Navy ships equipped with radio.

After a period of intense training exercises the four ships assigned to the 1st Division of the 1st Battle Squadron. In 1900, during the Boxer Rebellion in China the four ships had their first major operation, as they deployed to China in a gunboat diplomacy mission. Between 1901 and 1904 the four ships were taken at the KW Wilhelmshaven for reconstruction works. Part of the modernization was the addition of a second conning tower in the aft superstructure, as well as a gangway. Also, the boilers were replaced with newer ones, reducing the ships weight by 500 to 700 tons. The development of HMS Dreadnought in 1906, changed radical the landscape in the naval design. Dreadnought design followed two basic rules, heavy armament and steam turbine

**Ships**

| Name | Builder | Laid down | Launched | Completed | Fate |
|---|---|---|---|---|---|
| SMS Brandenburg | AG Vulcan, Stetin | 06/05/1890 | 21/11/1891 | 19/11/1893 | Scrapped, Danzig 1920 |
| SMS Wörth | Germaniawerft, Kiel | 06/04/1890 | 06/08/1892 | 31/10/1893 | Scrapped, Danzig 1919 |
| SMS Weissenburg Turgut Reiss (1910) | AG Vulcan, Stetin | 06/05/1890 | 14/12/1891 | 05/06/1894 | Demolished, Gölcük 1956 |
| SMS Elector Friedrich Wilhelm Hairedyn Barbaros (1910) | Wilhemshaven KW | 14/05/1890 | 30/06/1891 | 30/10/1893 | Sunk by HMS E11, on 08/08/1915 |

propulsion. All ships that did not follow these design principles called pre-dreadnoughts (including the *Brandenburg* class ships) and were considered obsolete, as the new *Dreadnought* class ships were introduced in the British and German navies. In 1907 the four ships decommissioned from the German Fleet. *In 1910 Weissenburg and Elector Friedrich Wilhelm were sold to the Ottoman Empire. The Ottomans, in a desperate effort to confront the Greek Navy that had been reinforced with the purchase of the armored cruiser G. Averof, bought the two most modern ships of the Brandenburg class.*

*In the beginning of WWI, Brandenburg and Wörth recommissioned and placed as coastal defense ships in the 5th Squadron serving in the Baltic and North Sea areas. With the end of WWI both ships were decommissioned again and scrapped in Danzig. Weissenburg was renamed as Turgut Reiss, and Elector Friedrich Wilhelm as Barbaros Hayreddin.* Both ships served in the Italo-Turkish war, in the Balkan Wars and in WWI but with poor results. The ships failed against *G. Averof* in the battles of *Elli* and *Lemnos*. In WWI, *Barbaross Hayredin* stayed strictly in the sea of Dardanelles and supported with his guns the Ottoman troops. The ship was sunk at August 8, 1915 by the British submarine *HMS E11*. *Turgut Reiss* also didn't see any real action during WWI. The most glorious moment for Turgut Reiss was in 25/01/1918 when she acted as a tug boat and helped the wounded and beached battlecruiser *Yavuz Sultan Selim* (*SMS Goeben*). *Turgut Reiss* remained as training ship until 1939, then as a barrack ship and finally demolished in 1957.

## Propulsion

In the end of 19th century triple expansion engines drove most warships. The *Brandenburgs* followed the rule, so they were equipped with two sets of 3-cylinder triple-expansion engines. Each set drove a 5m (diameter) 3 bladed screw. The machines were coal-fired by twelve transverse cylindrical boilers, with three fireboxes each. The twelve boilers (divided in two rooms), supplied 12 atmospheres pressurized steam to the engines. Each ship could carry 650 tons of coal, and in additional spaces up to 1050 tons. The ships were designed to achieve a speed of 16.5 knots (30.6km/h; 19mph). However, during the trials *Brandenburg* achieved a top speed of 16.3 knots (30.2 km/h; 18.8mph), while the other three ships achieved a maximum speed of 16.9 knots (31.3 km/h; 19.4mph). The maximum range of the ship was 4300 nautical miles (8000 km; 4900 miles) at 10 knots (19 km/h; 12mph) cruising speed. Also, the machines of the ship could provide up to 10000 metric horse-

power (9860 ihp; 7350 kw), but in practice the maximum horsepower varied from 9685 ihp (7223KW) from *Elector Friedrich Wilhelm, up to 10228 ihp (7627kW) for Wörth. Three generators (installations varied from ship to ship) were responsible for the electrical power with power ranged from 72.6 to 96.5 kilowatts.*

## Armament

The *Brandenburg* class ships were equipped with 28cm MRK (11" guns) as their primary armament. The ships adopted the six-gun configuration (in three twin gun turrets) rather than the typical four guns configuration of the pre-dreadnought battleships. However, the bow and stern turret carried 28cm with MRK L/40 barrel (gun length 11.2m), while the center turret carried the 28cm MRK L/35 guns with shorter barrel (gun length 9.8m). The shorter barrel adaptation for the midship turret was necessary in order to allow the rotation of the turret from side to side. However, the midship turret approach proved rather problematic as the guns were close enough to the deck and caused blast damages when fired. The 28 cm guns were mounted in Drh.L. C/92 type turrets, which provided elevation from −5 degrees to

25 degrees. The guns were capable of firing either armor-piercing (AP) or high explosive (HE) shells. At maximum elevation, they could hit targets out to 15900 m (17400 yards) with 250kg (529lbs) shells, while their effective range was 11000m (12030 yards). They could penetrate a side armor of 160mm at 12000 m (13120 yards). For the L/35 guns the maximum firing distance was 14400 m (15800 yards) and their effective range was 11000m (12030 yards. Their fire rate was rather low, i.e. 1 shell every 2 minutes, and this low fire rate explains the poor results for the *Brandenburgs* in the battles of *Elli* and *Lemnos*.

The secondary armament of the ships consisted of eight 10.5cm (4.1 in) SK L/35 guns. These quick-firing guns were mounted in open casemates in the front superstructure. Initially the ship was equipped with seven 10.5cm (4.1 in) SK L/35 guns, but after the 1901-1904 re-construction works one more gun was added. The 10.5 cm SK L/35 guns had a maximum firing distance of 10800 m (11810 yards) at 30.3 degrees of elevation. Practically they could fire up to 7.5 rounds per minute. Part of the secondary armament were also eight 8.8 cm (3.45 in) SK L/30 guns. Two of them were placed in forward sponsons, two in the forward superstructure, and four were emplaced around the rear superstructure. The 8.8 cm SK L/30 guns could fire up to 10500 m (11500 yards) with a rate of fire up to 15 rounds per minute. Like all other battleships of this era, the *Brandenburgs* were also armed with six 45 cm torpedo tubes and 16 torpedoes. Two of them were mounted in the bow and four in the stern.

## Protection

*In 1890, Harvey armour from Harvey United Steel Company was monopolizing the ships construction & armour business. The Harvey process consisted in carburizing (cementing) the face of a nickel-steel plate by heating it and holding then the plate in high temperature for a long period. The Krupp process was a variant of Harvey processes, as the Germans added 1% chromium for additional hardness. The ballistic tests quickly showed the superiority of Krupp process, as 25.9cm of Krupp armour offered the same protection as 30.4 cm of Harvey armour, and all the major navies adopted the Krupp armour. From the four ships only Weissenburg and Elector Friedrich Wilhelm were armored with Krupp armour. The other two ships (Brandenburg and Wörth) were armored with the less effective composite armour due to delivery problems from Krupp, as Krupp armour effectively provided twice the amount of protection. The composite armor was a layered armour from steel plates and wooden planks, which was backed by two more layers of sheet iron. However, some parts of Brandenburg did receive the new Krupp armor, including the barbettes of the fore and center main turrets. The armour of the ships was varying from the hull to the superstructure. The hull protection above the waterline was protected by an armored belt. The belt was 400mm in the center and tapered gradually to 300mm. Below the water line the belt was starting from 200mm and tapered to both ends to 180mm. The Brandenburgs had a 60  mm thick armored deck.  Also, the barbettes had 300 mm protection and were backed with 210 mm of wood.*

## Career

Upon their commissioning, the *Bradenburgs* followed an intense training exercises program in the Baltic sea. However, the service life of *SMS Brandenburg* was marked by a lethal event. During testing on 16 February 1894, a stem pipe exploded while the ship was docked in *Strander Bucht*. The explosion killed 25 men of the crew plus 18 dockyard workers. After two months the repair works for the ship completed, and finally *Brandenburg* and the three other ships joined the 1st division of the 1st Battle Squadron of *Kaiserliche Marine*.

In 1897, two German missionaries assassinated in China. Germany took advantage of this assassination and in 15 January 1898 forced the government of China to lease it an area of 553 square kilometers for 99 years. This area around the city oh Qingdao was the first European colony on mainland China, as Hong Kong (Britain) and Macau (Portugal) were all islands. In 1900, during the Boxer Rebellion, Chinese nationalists attacked western embassies in Beijing and murdered the German

attaché *Clemens von Ketteler*. These acts of violence against Westerners in China led to the colonial powers to form an alliance between them and to send troops and ships in China. The Germans had already 2000 men in China along with the East Asia Squadron. The East Asia Squadron consisted by the protected cruisers *Kaiserin Augusta*, *Hansa*, and *Hertha* and the gunboats *Jaguar* and *Iltis*. Kaiser decided to reinforce the East Asia Squadron by sending (under the commands of Alfred von Waldersee), a flotilla with the Brandenburgs, six cruisers, and six marine regiments. The ships left Germany on 11 July, stopped for coal supplies in Gibraltar and passed the Suez Canal on 26-27 July.  After coal resupplies the fleet entered the Indian Ocean. They arrived on 30 August (passing through Singapore and Hong-Kong), outside of Shanghai. However, when the German fleet finally arrived too late, as the rebellion of Boxers in Beijing was already suppressed by other Alliance troops. Brandenburg started to patrol in the estuary of Yangtze river. After several months of inaction as the ships sent to Hong-Kong and Nagasaki for minor repairs, the fleet was ordered (on 26 May) to return to Germany. On August 11, 1901 the ships arrived back in Germany and the expeditionary fleet was dissolved. The whole operation was criticized inside Germany mainly by Admiral *Tirpitz*, as the operation costed to the German government more than 100 million marks.

After their return to Germany the ships moved to KW Wilhelmshaven for reconstruction works until 1904. During the reconstruction operations the boilers were replaced, a second coning tower was added in the aft superstructure, one more rapid-fire gun (8.8 cm SK L/35) was added, while the coal storage capacity increased. The ships were recommissioned in 1905 and transferred to the North Sea Reserve Formation acting as coastal defense ships. Finally, the ships were decommissioned in September 1907. In 1909 the Ottoman Turks after the acquisition of the *Pisa* class armored cruiser *G. Averof* by the Greek Navy, asked the British government for the modernization of the Ottoman Navy. The British offered two *Royal Sovereign* class ships. As the Turks rejected the offer, they started conversations with the German military attaché in Constantinople. Initially the Turks interested to buy one or two new battlecruisers (*Moltke, Göeben*). Because the Ottoman fleet was headed by British Admiral the Germans refused to sell their new battleships as they did not want their naval technology to come in British hands. Instead they offered the four *Brandenburgs* to the Ottomans at a cost of 10 million marks. Finally, the Ottomans choose to buy *SMS Weissenburg*, and *SMS Elector Friedrich Wilhelm* plus several new destroyers *(S165, S166, S167 & S168). The ships were transferred on 1 September 1910 and were renamed as Barbaross Hayreddin and Turgut Reiss. However, both vessels appeared problematic. First, there was no trained personnel and the Turks used enlisted men from the rest of their fleet. Their rangefinders have been removed, some pumps and pipes were rusted, while the telephone system was not operational. The outcome of these technical problems was the reduction of their cruising speed from 10 to 8 knots.*

*The ships like the majority of the Ottoman fleet remained in the safety f the Dardanelles sea during the Italo-Turkish war of 1911-1912. In the Balkan*

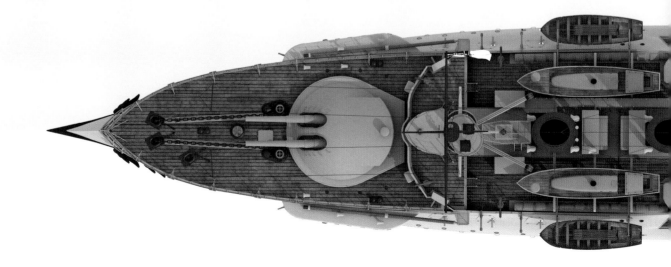

wars (1912 - 1913) when the Balkan League declared war against the Ottoman Empire, both ships bombarded the Bulgarian troops in Varna and participated in the blockade of Varna port. In December of 1912, the Ottoman fleet was reorganized and Hayredinn Barbaross was named as the flagship of the fleet. The Ottomans attempted to break the Greek blockade of the Dardanelles sea. They engaged with the Greeks in the Battle of Elli (16 December 1912). In the battle the Ottoman flagship was hit twice. The Greek battleship G. Averof bombarded Barbaross and a shell killed five sailors in the rear deck, while another hit damaged the rear turret. After the battle, the Ottoman ship remained blockaded in the Dardanelles. One month later in a second attempt (Battle of Lemnos), Turks tried again without success to break the Greek blockade and to sink G. Averof. During the battle the amidships turret of Brabaross was destroyed (again by G. Averof) and all the men inside the turret were killed. Both Brandenburgs fired up to 800 shells against the Greek fleet without any success. After the failure against the Greek fleet the two ships moved to the safe waters of Black sea supporting again the Turkish troops against the Bulgarian army. In the beginning of WWI Barbaross was under repair works. The ships bombarded the British and Australian troops during the Gallipoli campaign (25 April 1915). However, Barbaross 30 minutes later retired from the bombardment, as after firing fifteen shells, the right gun of the center turret exploded and destroyed the gun. Two months later a similar accident happened as a shell exploded inside one of Turgut Reis's guns. As a result, both ships were withdrawn. On 8 August 1915 Barbaross was intercepted by the British submarine HMS E11 in Bolayır in the Sea of Marmara. Barbaross was sunk by a single torpedo hit, killing 21 officers and 237 men of the crew.

Turgut Reiss stayed in the Golden Horn in Constantinople after the sunk of Barbaross and some of his guns were removed and placed in the Dardanelles. On 19 January 1918, the battleship Yavuz (Goeben) and the light cruiser Berslau (Midilli) after a raid against British ships in Northern Aegean returned back in Dardanelles. Midilli struck five mines and sank, and Yavuz hit three mines and stack. Three days later Turgut Reiss tried to free Yavuz from the sand bank and finally escorted with success the battleship Yavuz back in Constantinople.

After the end of WWI and in the Treaty of Sevres (1920) Turgut Reiss was offered to Japan as the allies decided to divide the Ottoman fleet. The Japanese government rejected the offer of Turgut Reiss, and as the tensions between Greeks and Turks escalated, the Treaty of Sevres ceased to apply and in 1923 the Treaty of Lausanne was signed, and the ship remained in Turkish hands. She served as a stationary training ship in the naval base of Gölcük, and finally demolished in 1957.

In the beginning of WWI, the other two ships SMS Brandenburg and SMS Worth recommissioned in the V Squadron as coastal defense ships. Brandenburg was acquired by the Ottomans in 1915 as the Ottomans wanted to use their guns for defense of the Dardanelles, but she never transferred. After the end of WWI in May 1919, the two ships decommissioned from the German Navy and finally moved to Danzig where they scrapped between 1919 and 1920. In general, the Brandenburg class was an innovative class of ships for the decade of 1890, but the rapid development of naval technology mainly with the appearance of HMS Dreadnought, made these ships and all the pre-Dreadnought ships obsolete.

## Bibliography

Nottelmann, Dirk. Die Brandenburg-Klasse: Höhepunkt des deutschen Panzerschiffbaus Hamburg 2002, Verlag A.S. Mittler, ISBN 3813207404

Sondhaus, Lawrence. Preparing for Weltpolitik: German Sea Power Before the Tirpitz Era. Annapolis, 1997, Naval Institute Press. ISBN 9781557507457

Fotakis, Zhshs. Greek Naval Strategy and Policy 1910–1919, London and New York, Routledge 2005

Weir, Gary E. Building the Kaiser's Navy: The Imperial Navy Office and German Industry in the Tirpitz Era, 1890–1919. Annapolis 1992: Naval Institute Press. ISBN 9781557509291.

Langensiepen, Bernd, and Ahmet Güleryüz. The Ottoman Steam Navy, 1828–1923, Annapolis: Naval Institute Press, 1995.

Grießmer, Axel, Die Linienschiffe der Kaiserlichen Marine. Bonn 1999, Bernard & Graefe Verlag, ISBN 978-3-7367-5985-9

**General characteristics**

| | |
|---|---|
| Type of vessel: | battleship |
| Class: | Brandenburg class |
| Crew: | 568-591 man |
| Ships | SMS Brandenburg, SMS Weissenburg (Turgut Reiss), SMS Wörth, SMS Elector Friedrich Wilhem (Barbaros Heyreddin) |

**Technical data**

| | |
|---|---|
| Design Displacement: | 10013 tons |
| Maximum use displacement: | 10670 tons |
| Length: | overall: 113,9 m above everything: 115,7 m |
| Width: | 19,5 m |
| Draught: | 7,4 m |
| Machinery: | 12 transverse cylinder boilers with coal firing; 2 x 3-Cylinder Triple Expansion steam engines |
| Number of screws: | 2 x 3 blade screws with diameter 5,0 m |
| Wave Speed: | 109/min |
| Performance: | 9.886 PSI |
| Maximum Speed: | 16,9 knots |
| Range: | 4.300 nautical miles with a cruising speed of 10 knots |
| Fuel Supply: | Max. 1050 tons of coal |

**Armour**

| | |
|---|---|
| Belt Tanks: | 305-406 mm |
| Deck: | 60 mm |
| Towers: | 127 mm |

**Control Room**

| | |
|---|---|
| Horizontal: | 30 mm |
| Vertical: | 300 mm |
| Bar Beds: | 300 mm steel |

**Armament**

| | |
|---|---|
| Primary Guns: | 4 × 28 cm (MRK L/40); 2 × 28cm (MRK L/35); Coat ring cannons in three turrets with total. 352 shot, range 28 cm: 15,9 km |
| Secondary Guns: | 8 × 10.5 cm SK L/35 Rapid fire guns in open casemates with total 600 shot; 8(7+1) × 8.8 cm SK L/35 Rapid fire guns with total 2000 shot; 4× 3,7 cm guns |
| Tubes: | 6 × 45cm torpedo tubes with 16 torpedoes, (four in the stern, two in the bow) all above the water line |

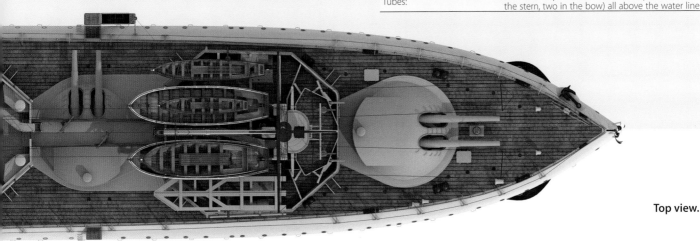

Top view.

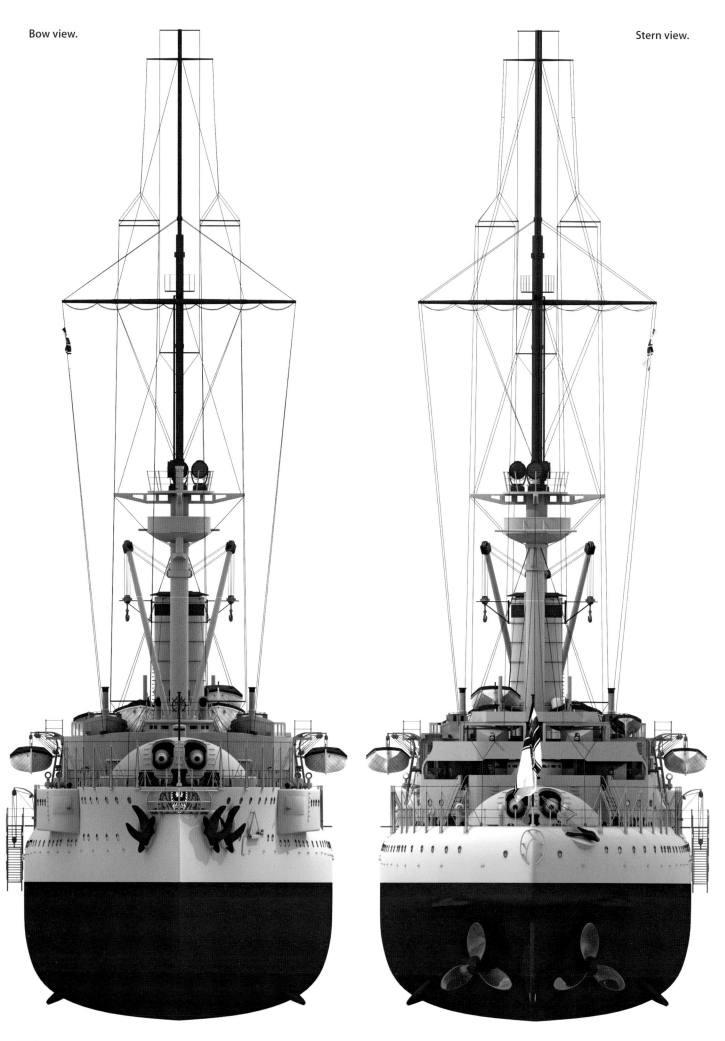

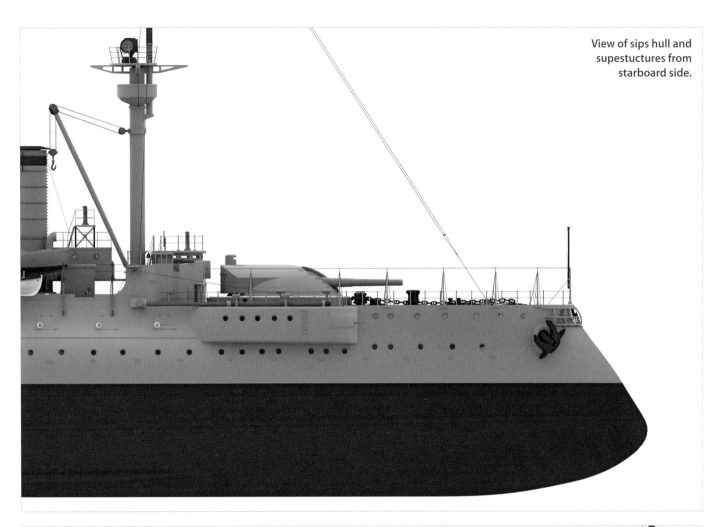

View of sips hull and supestuctures from starboard side.

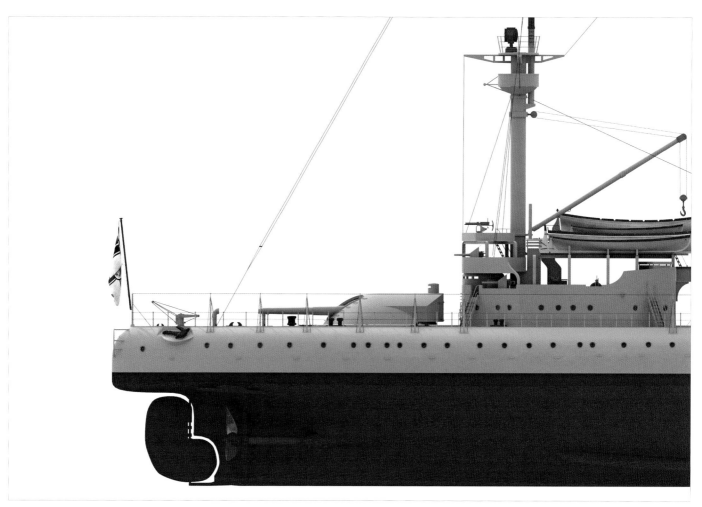

View of sips hull and supestuctures from
port side.

View of sips hull and supestuctures from top.

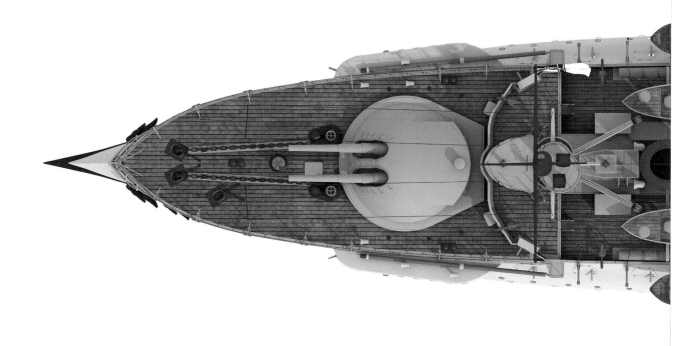

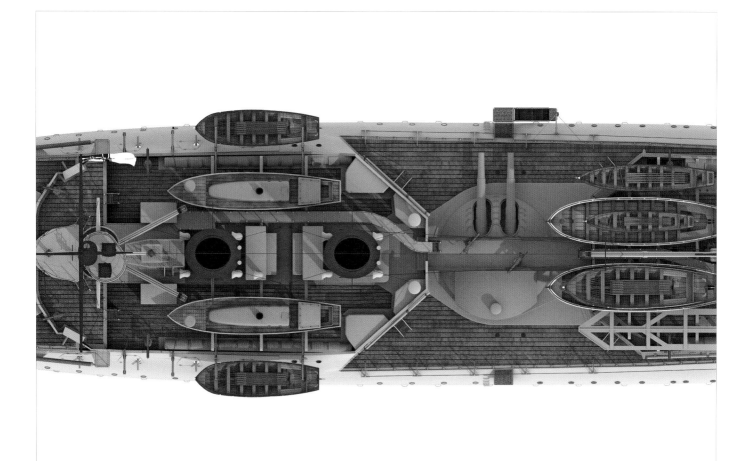

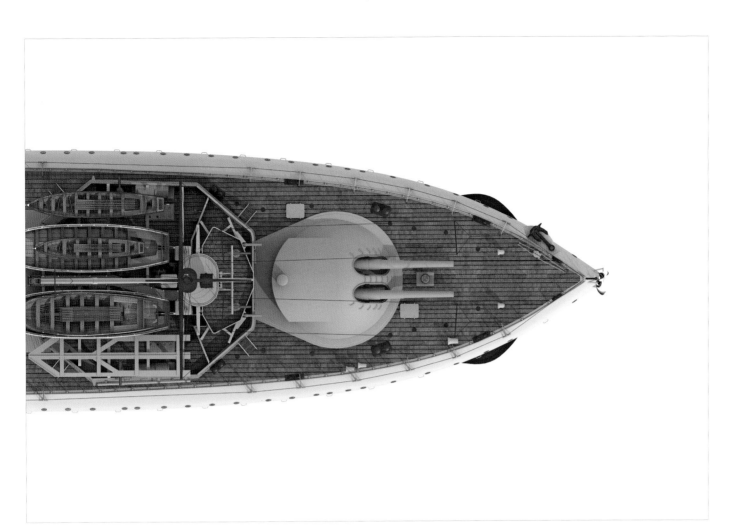

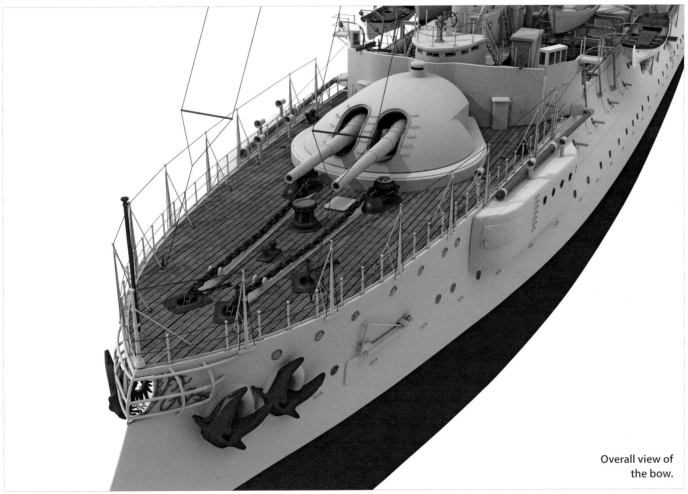

Overall view of
the bow.

Overall view of
the bow.

Forecastle deck with
te ancors, chains and
capstans.

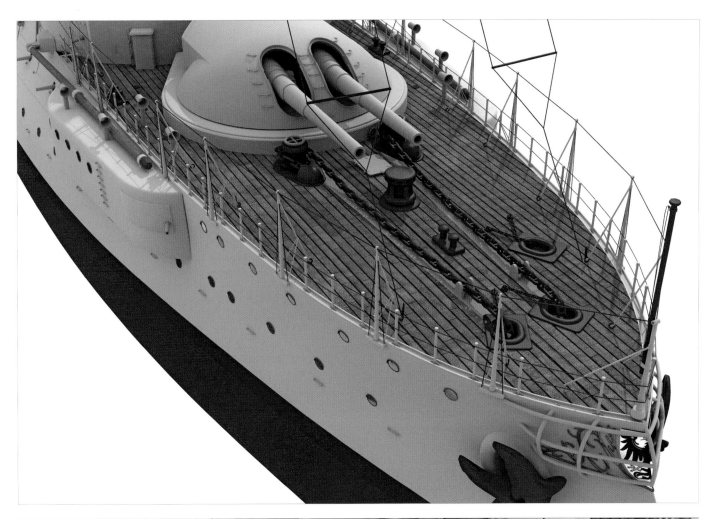

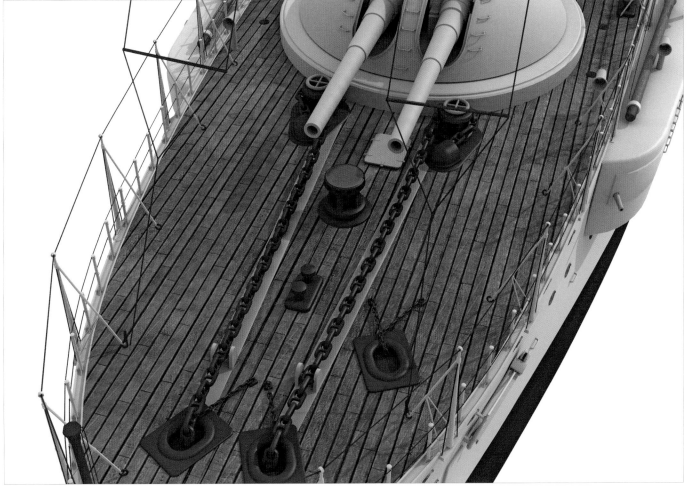

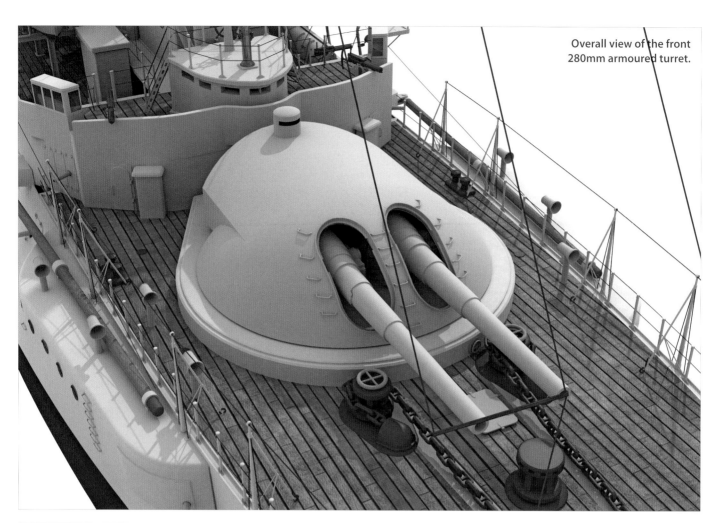
Overall view of the front 280mm armoured turret.

Views of the front 280mm armoured turret.

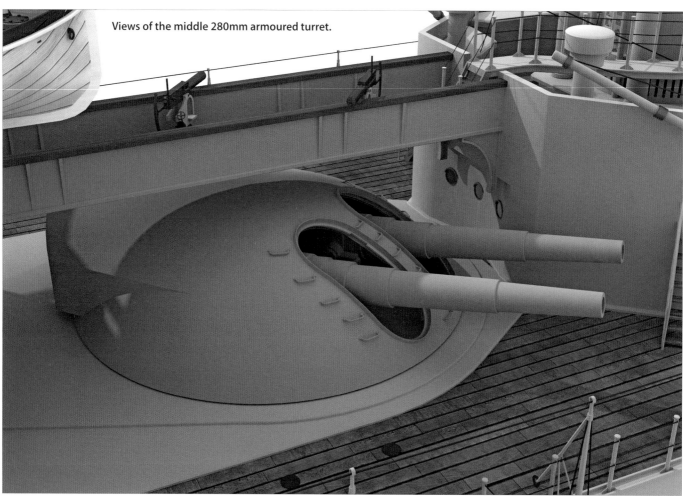

Views of the middle 280mm armoured turret.

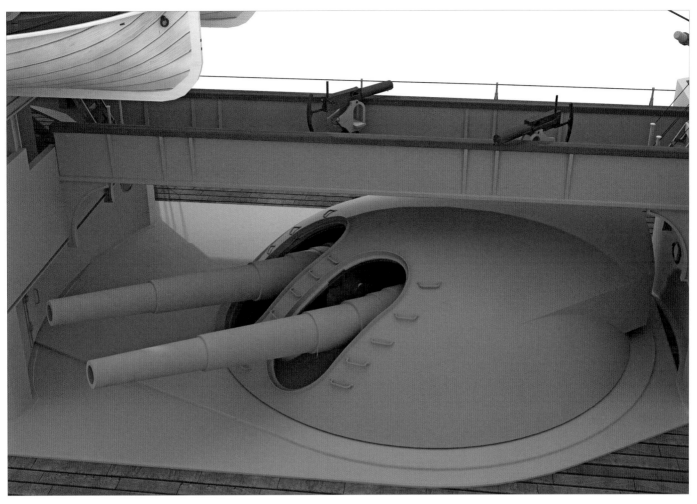

Views of the rear 280mm armoured turret.

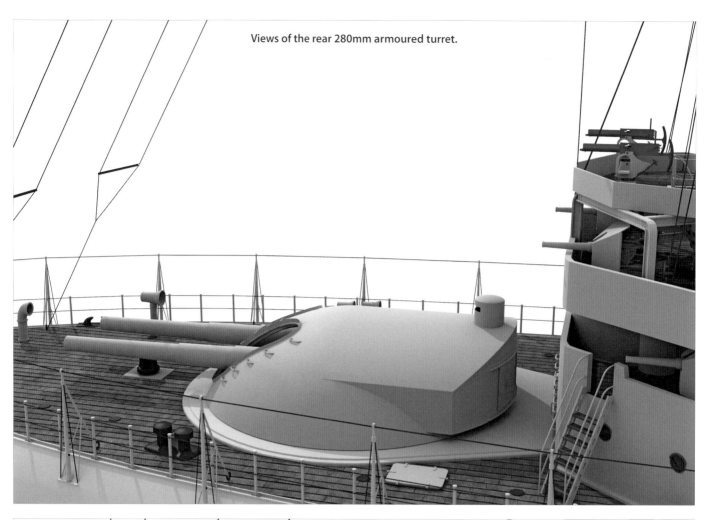

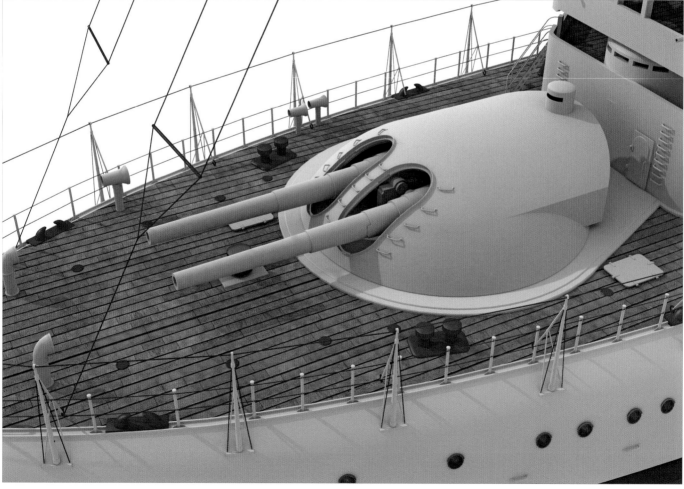

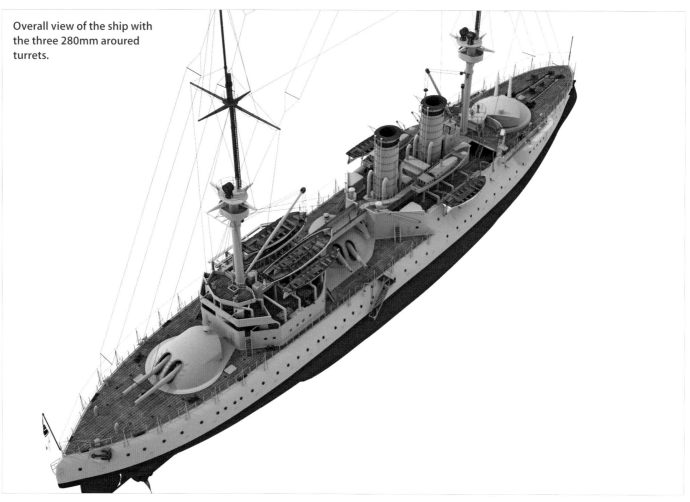

Overall view of the ship with the three 280mm aroured turrets.

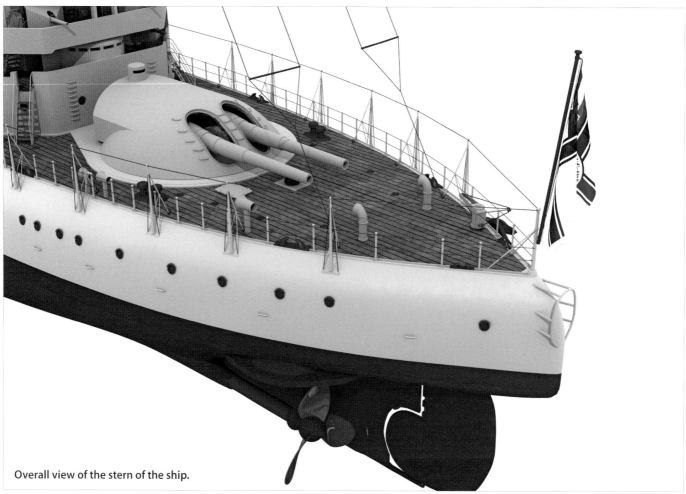

Overall view of the stern of the ship.

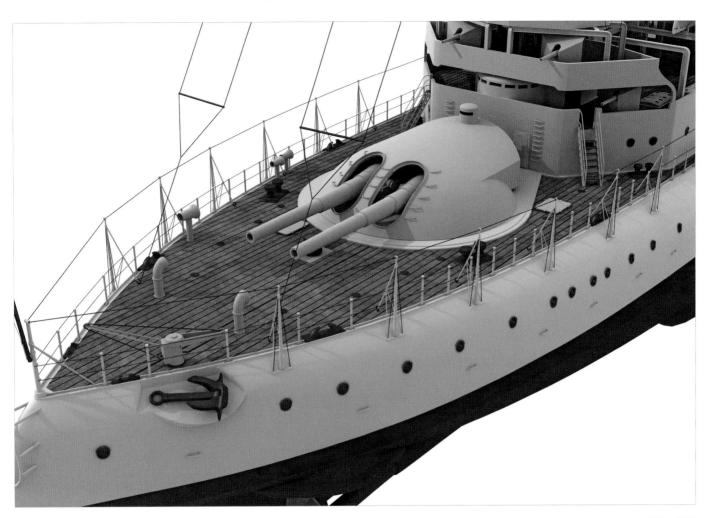

View of the stern crane and the additional rear anchor.

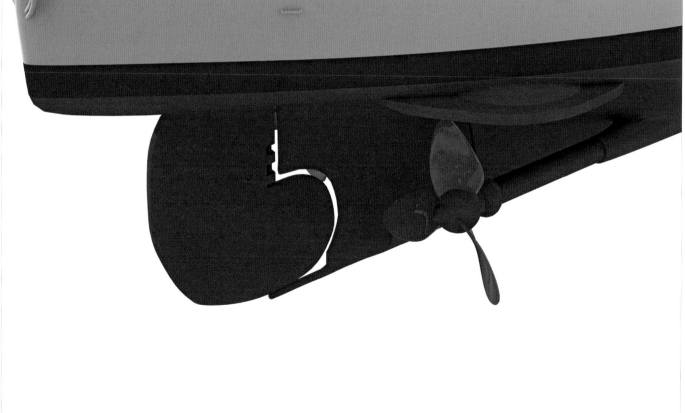

View of the rudder and the propelers of the ship.

Views of the rear superstructure of the ship.

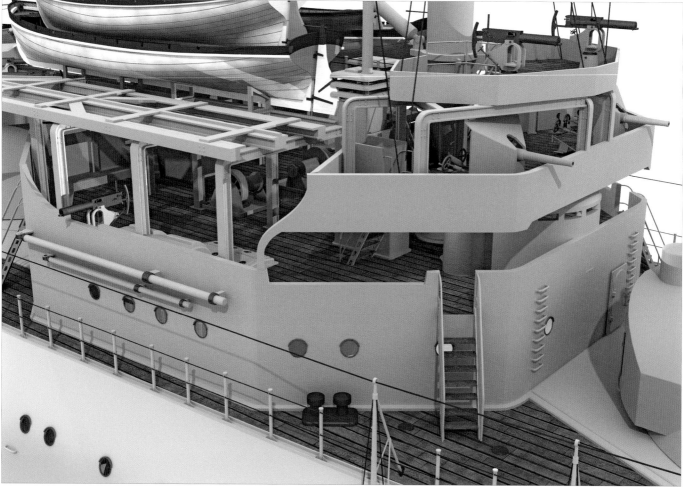

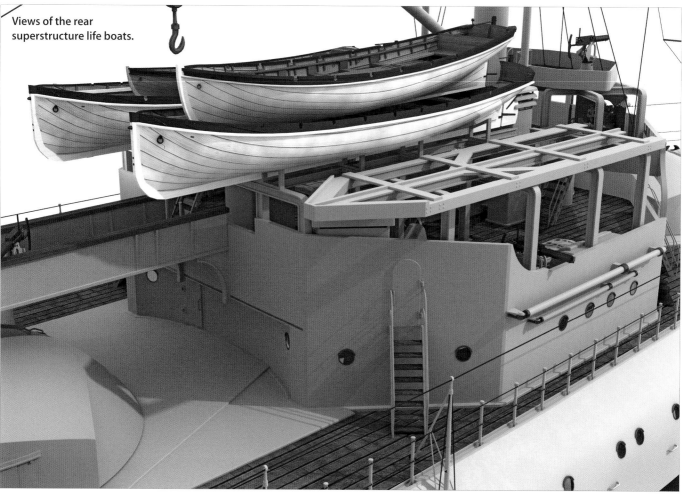

Views of the rear
superstructure life boats.

Views of the rear superstructure mounting framework for the life boats.

View of te stern of te sip from the rear supestructure upper deck.

View of the additional corridor over the mounting life boat framework.

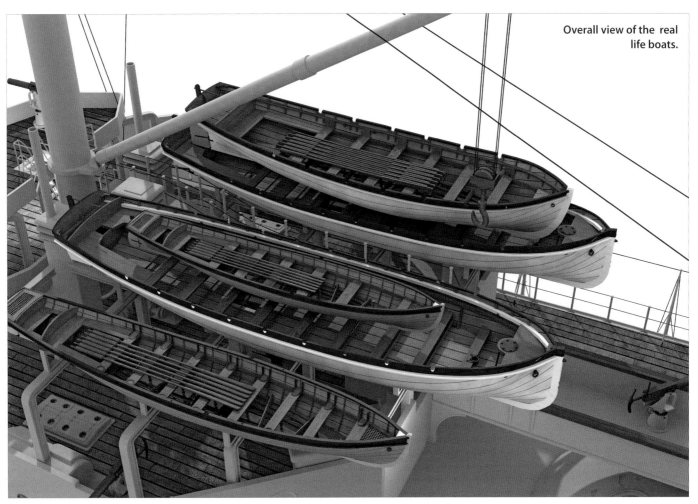

Overall view of the real life boats.

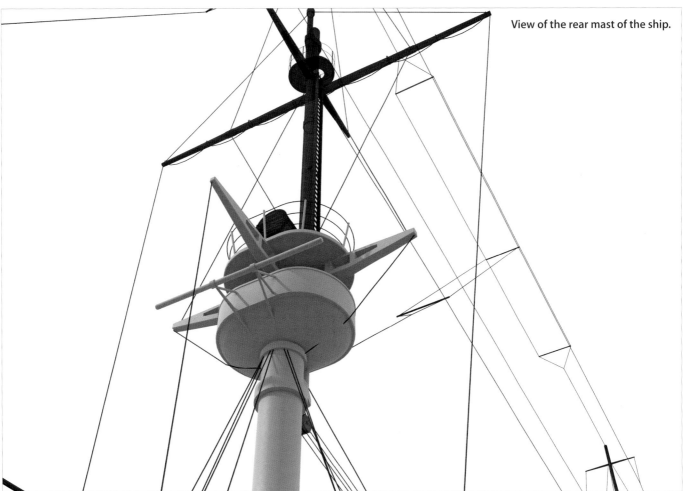

View of the rear mast of the ship.

Views of the ship from
the rear mast search light
position.

View of the additional corridor in the main supestructure of the ship.

View of the 105mm L/35 QF guns installation in te main deck of the ship.

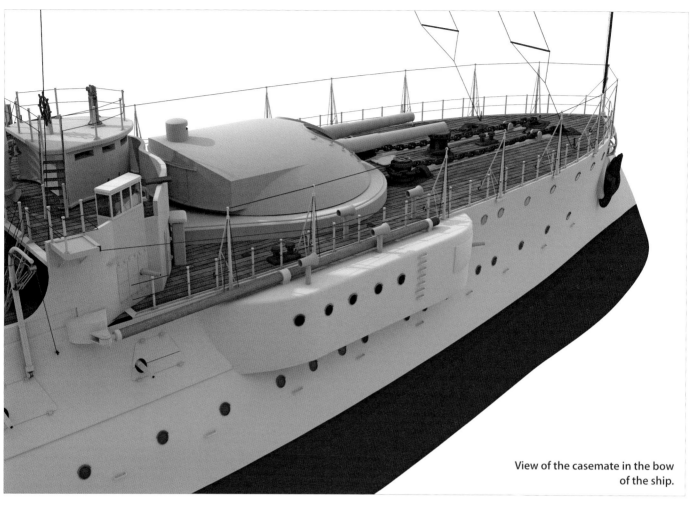

View of the casemate in the bow
of the ship.

View of the main superstructure mounting framework for the life boats.

View of the main battlestation of the ship.

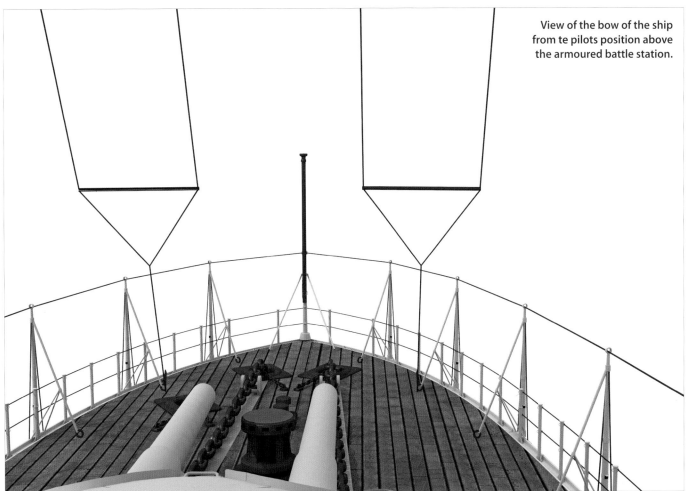

View of the bow of the ship from te pilots position above the armoured battle station.

View of the front mast of the ship.

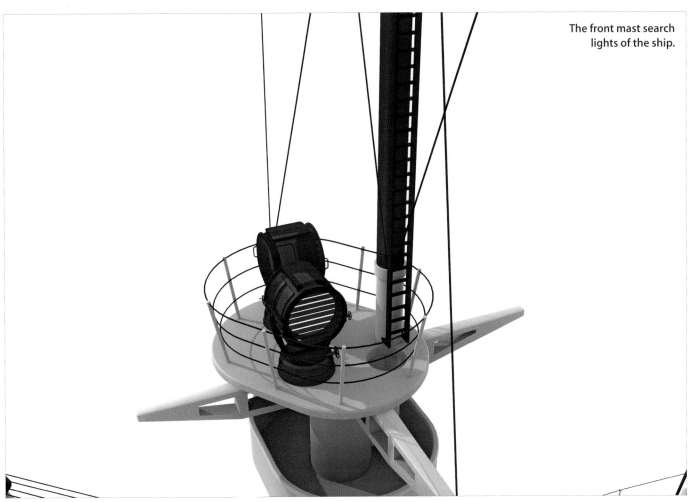

The front mast search lights of the ship.

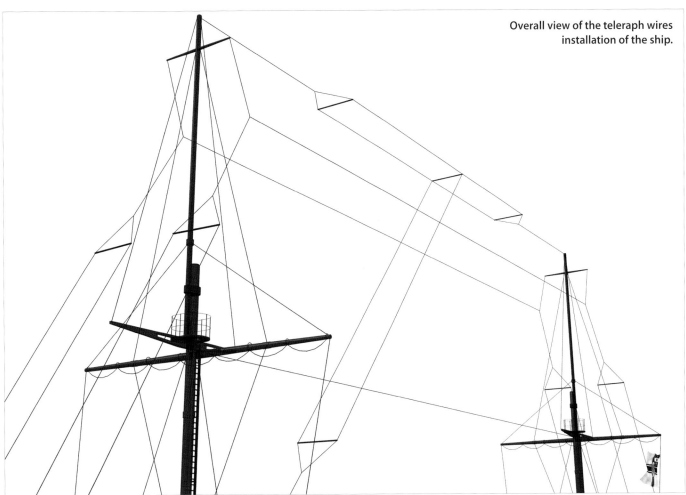

Overall view of the teleraph wires installation of the ship.

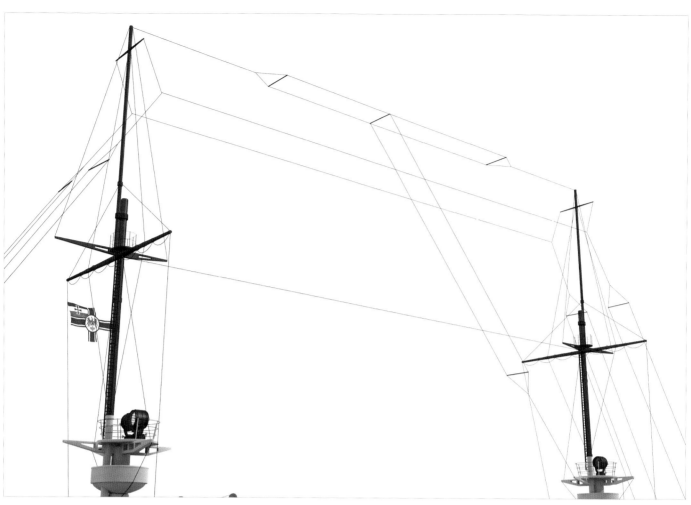

Overall view of the funnels of the ship.

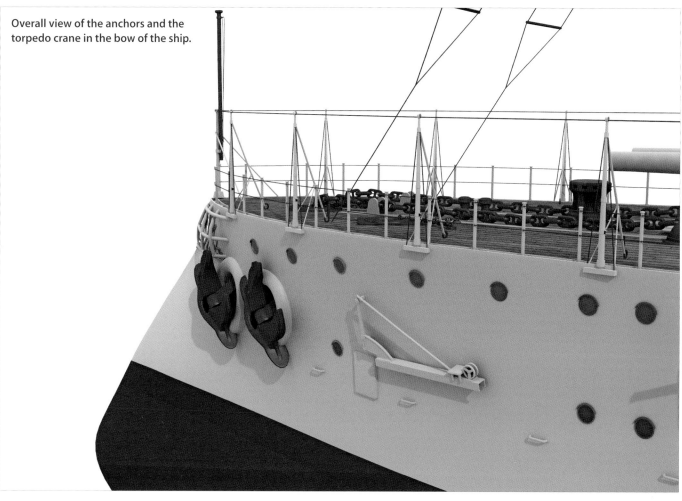

Overall view of the anchors and the torpedo crane in the bow of the ship.

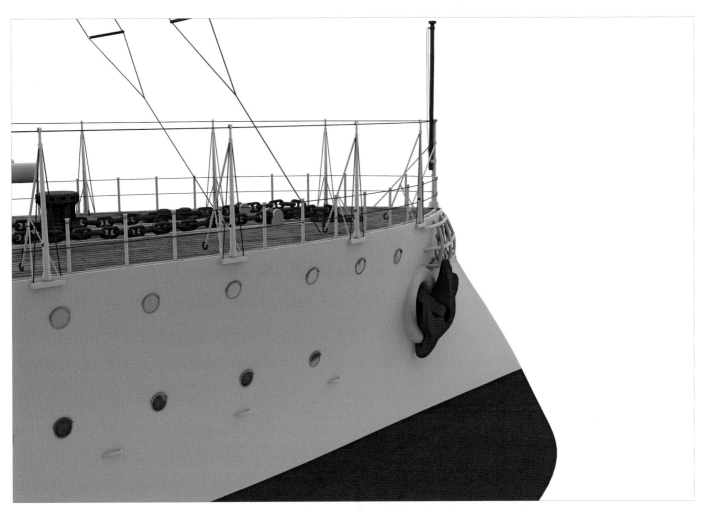

Overall view of the ganway in the middle of the ship.

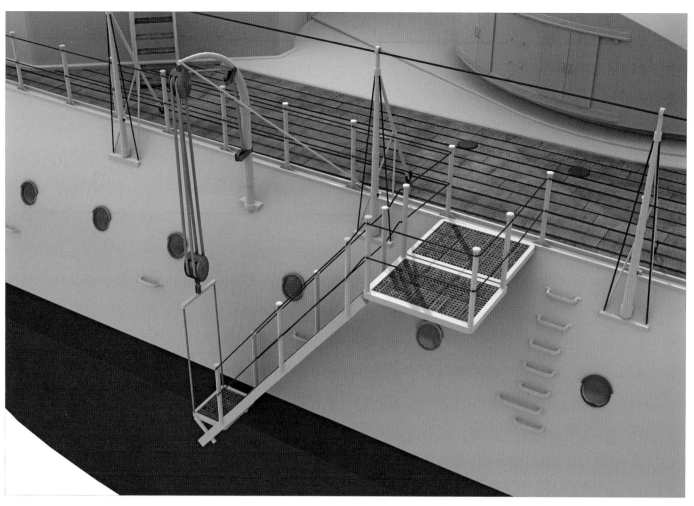

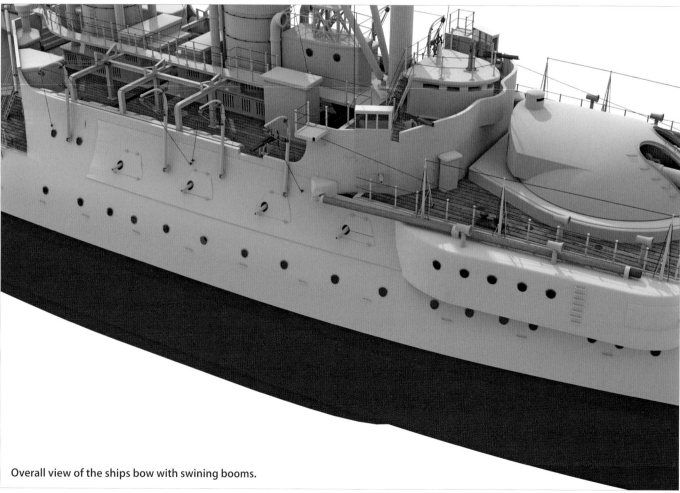

Overall view of the ships bow with swining booms.

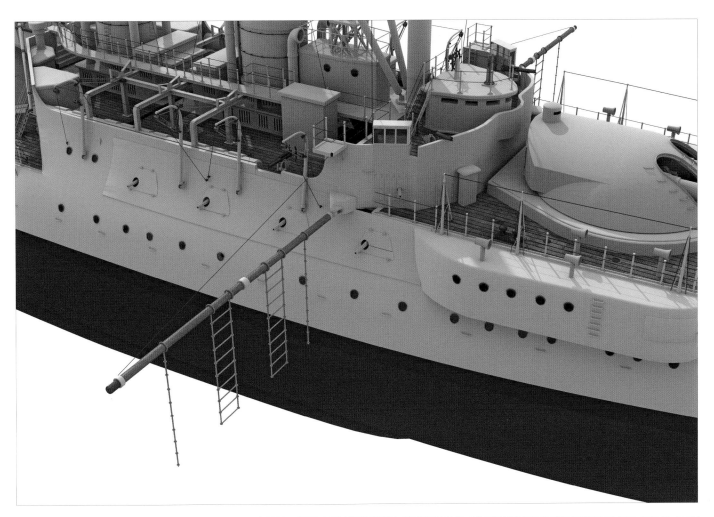

Overall view of the funnels of the
ship and of the front mast crane
control platform.

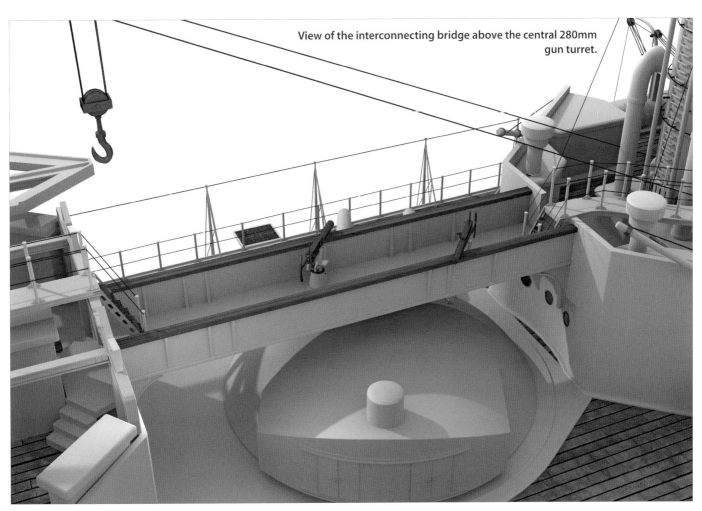

View of the interconnecting bridge above the central 280mm gun turret.

Views of the 37mm QFC gun.

Overall view of the main deck life boat cranes.

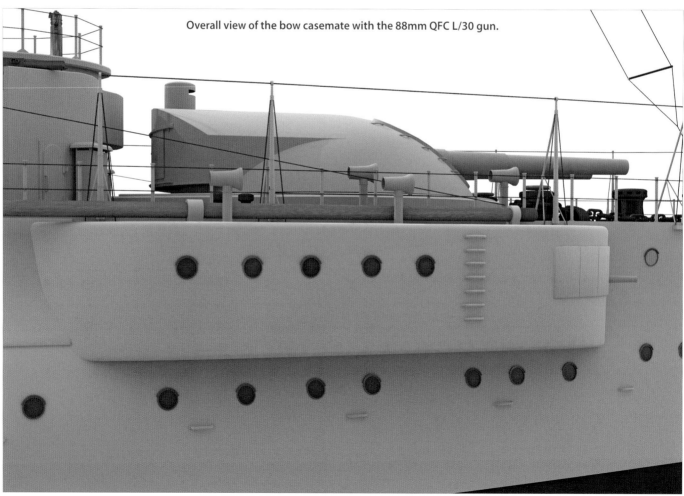

Overall view of the bow casemate with the 88mm QFC L/30 gun.

Overall view of the (4+4) 105mm QFC SL/35 guns.

Views of the 105mm SL/35 QFC guns.

Overall view of the deck casemate with the 88mm QFC gun.

Views of the life boats of the ship.

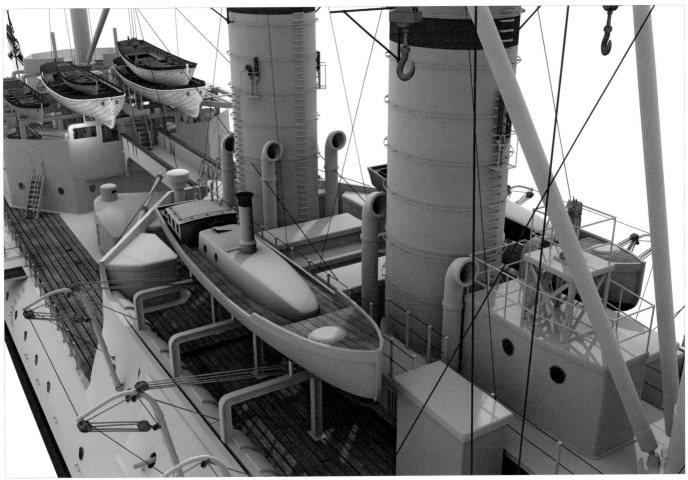

View of the superstructure of the ship with the steam pinnaces.

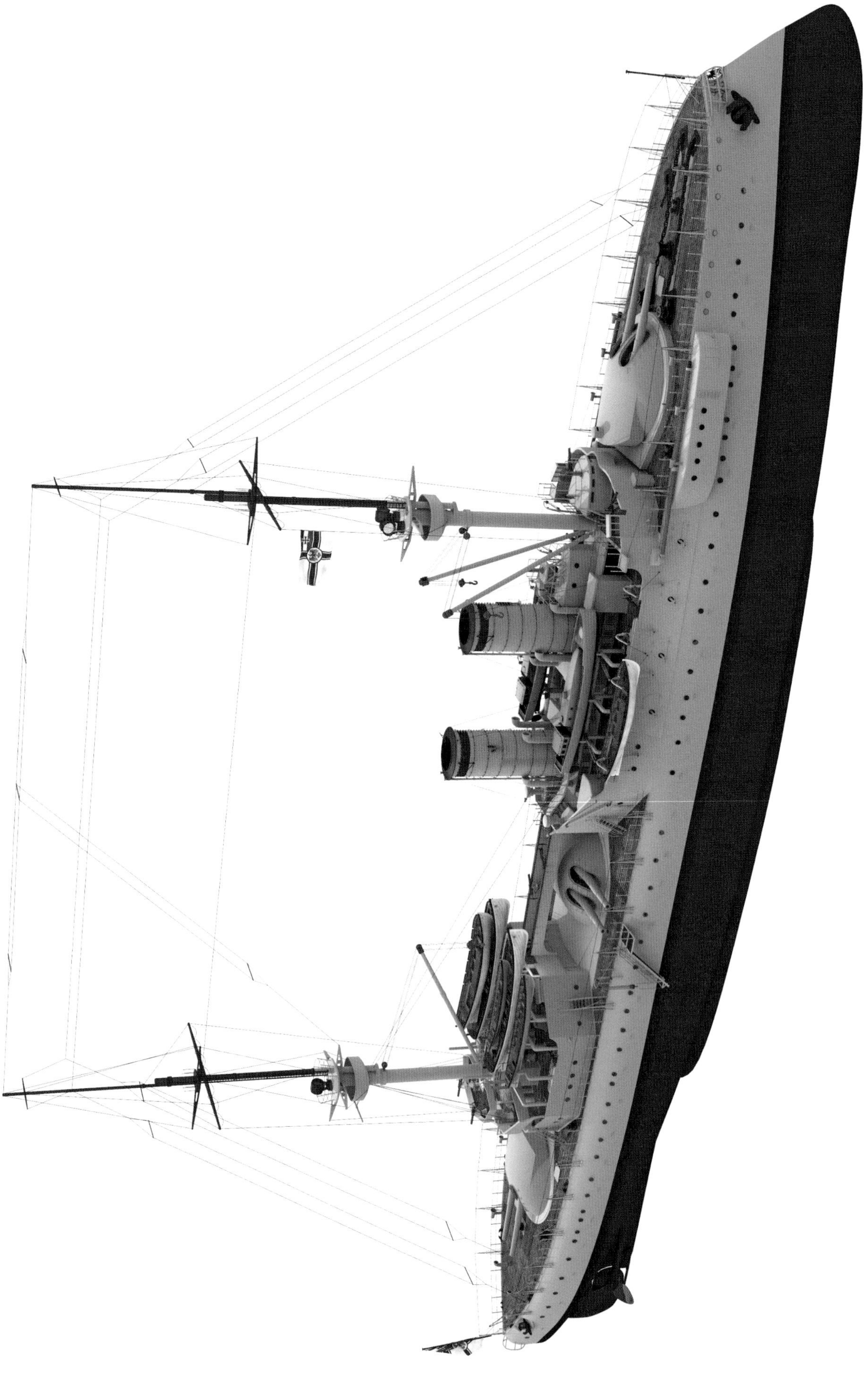

Overall view of the ship.

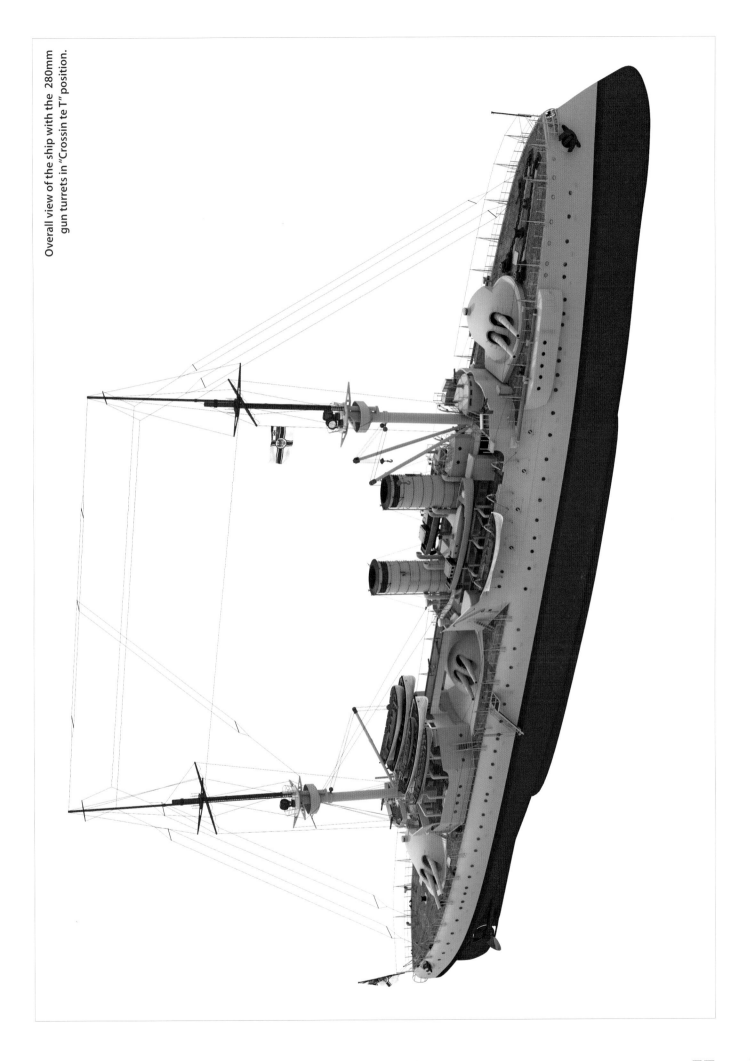

Overall view of the ship with the 280mm gun turrets in "Crossing the T" position.

Overall view of the ships bow.

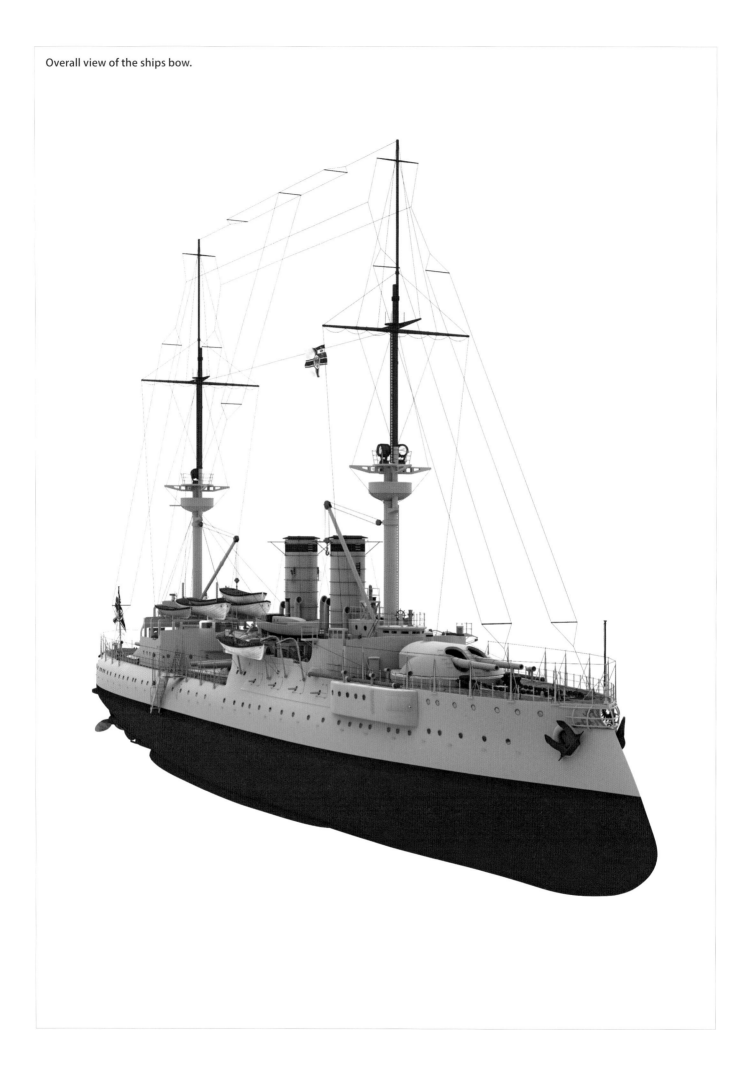

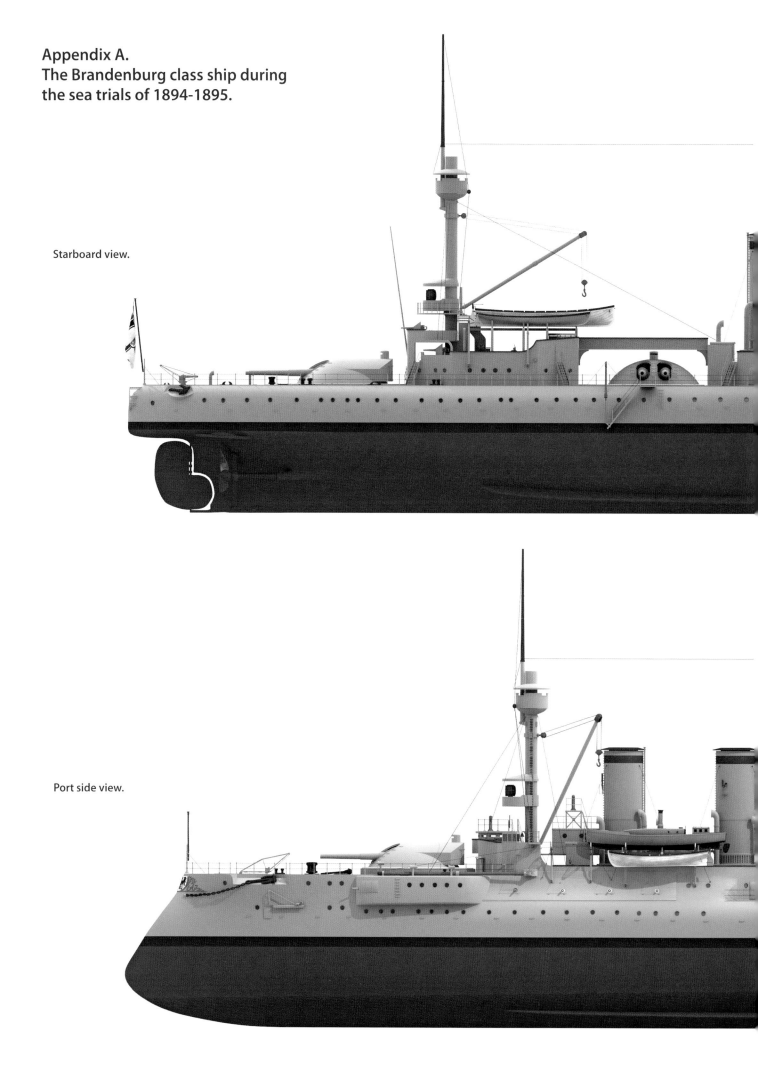

**Appendix A.**
The Brandenburg class ship during
the sea trials of 1894-1895.

Starboard view.

Port side view.

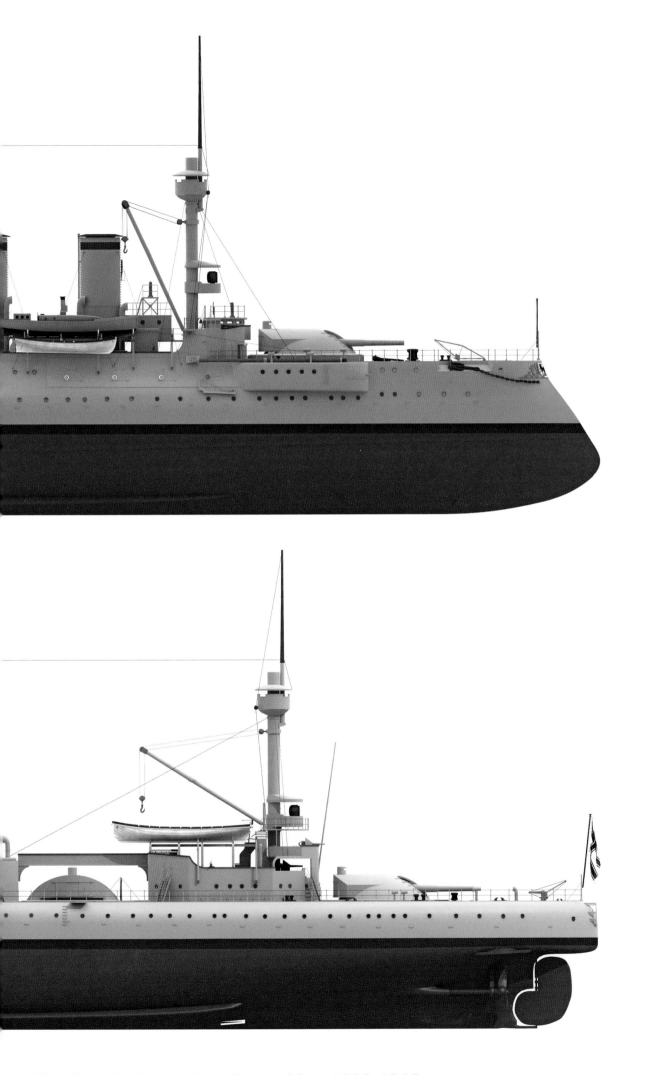

Top view.

Bow view of the ship.

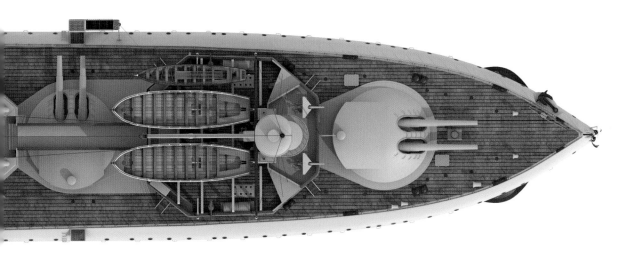

Stern view of the ship.

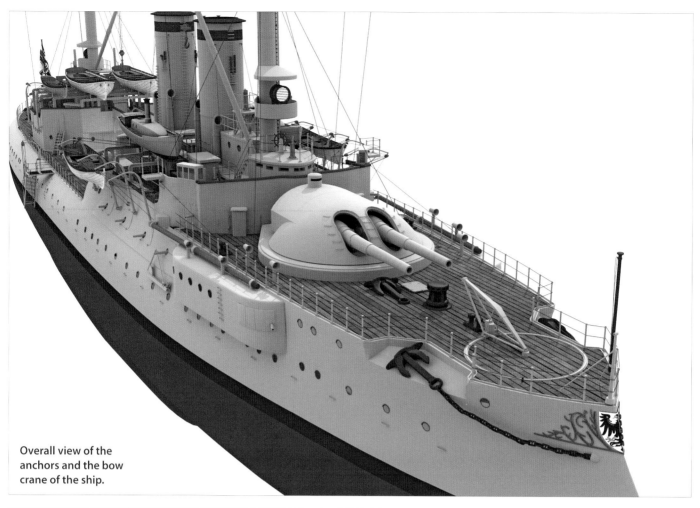

Overall view of the
anchors and the bow
crane of the ship.

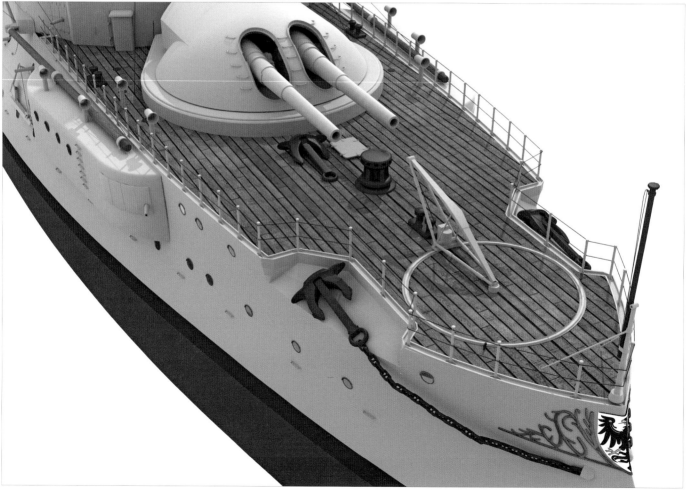

Overall view of rear superstructure and the search light of the ship.

Overall view of the mounting framework in the rear superstructure of the ship.

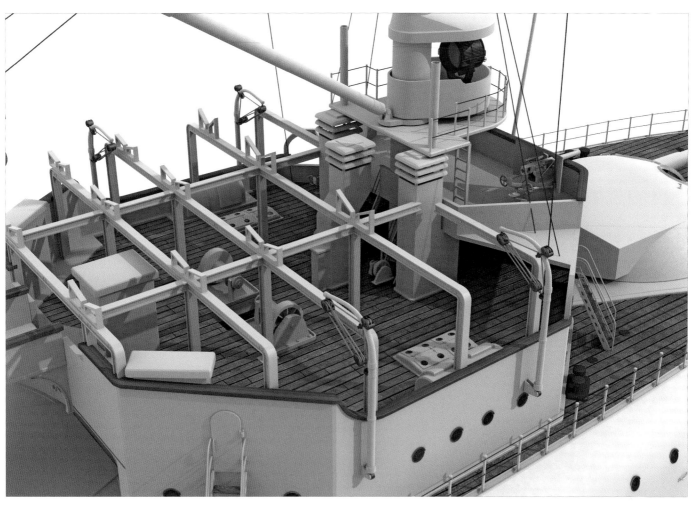

Views of the initial telergraph wires installation.

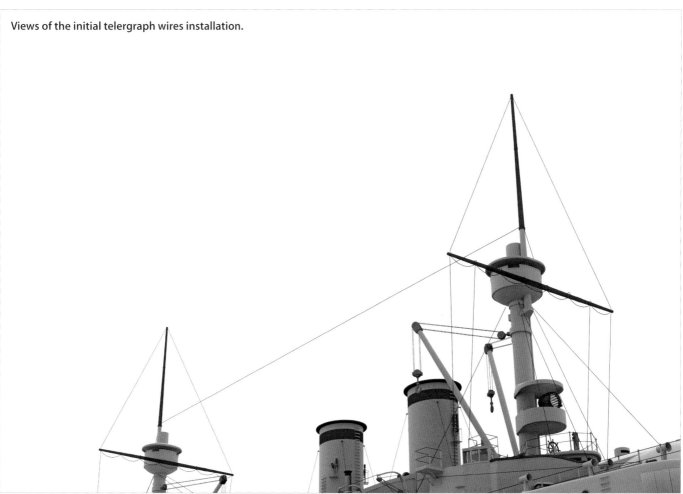

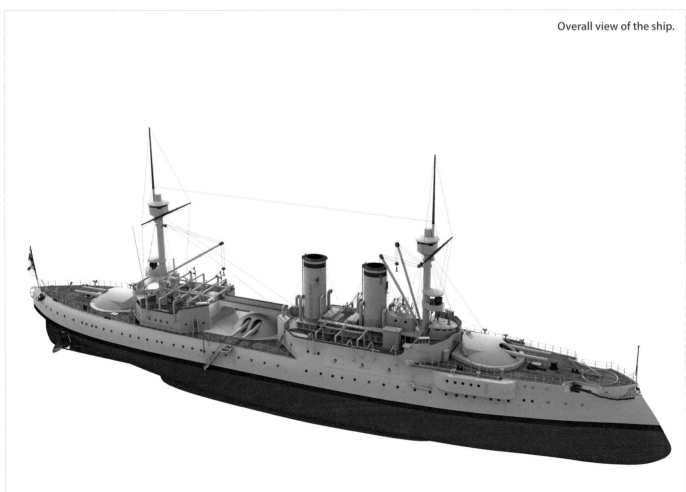

Overall view of the ship.

View if the initial (3+3) 105mm gun installation.

View of the auxilliary life boat cranes in te rear part of the ship.

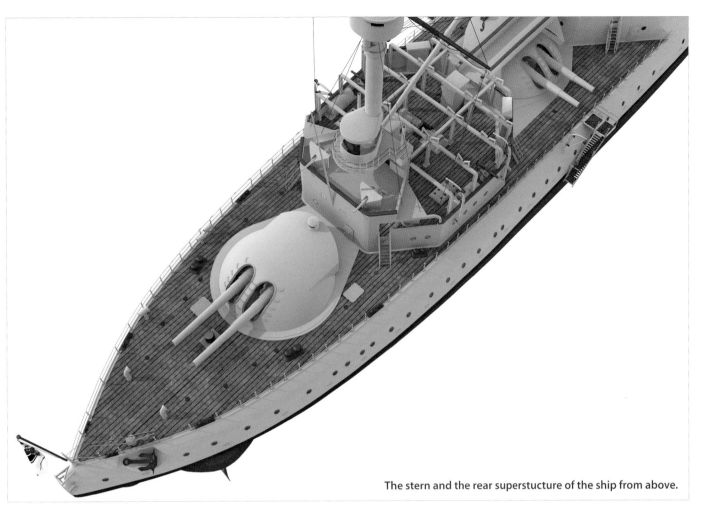

The stern and the rear superstucture of the ship from above.

The bow and the front superstucture
of the ship from above.

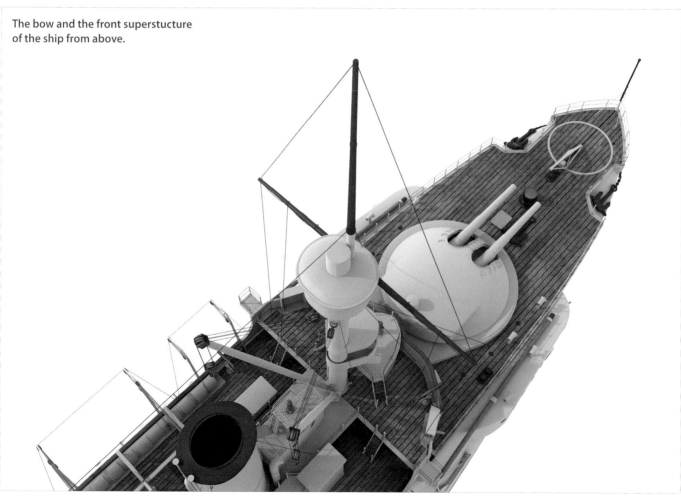

Bird-eye view of the ship.

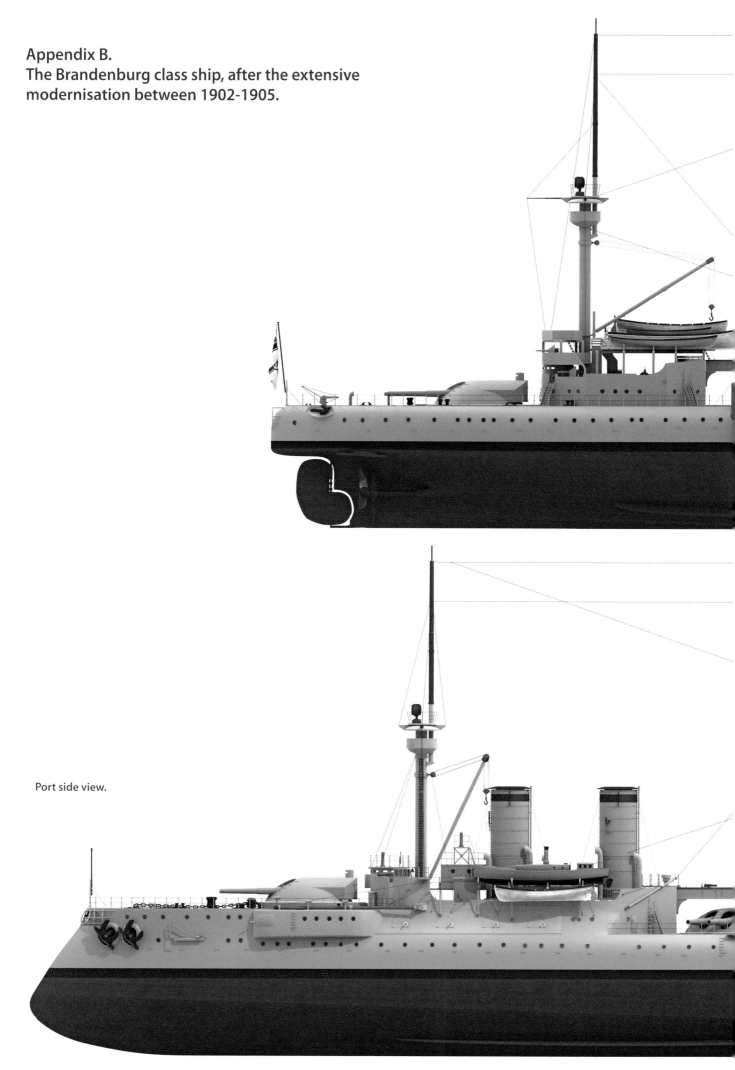

Appendix B.
The Brandenburg class ship, after the extensive
modernisation between 1902-1905.

Port side view.

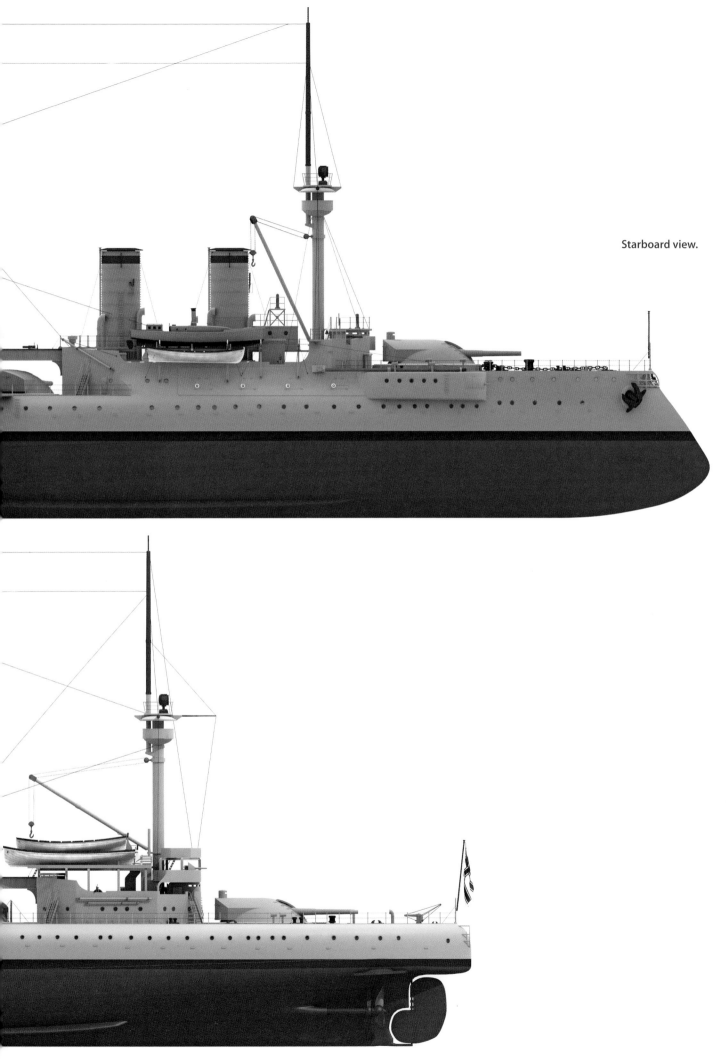

Starboard view.

Top view.

Bow view of the ship.

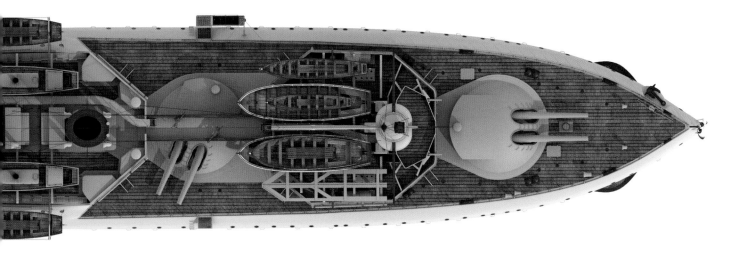

Stern view of the ship.

Views of the initial telergraph wires installation.

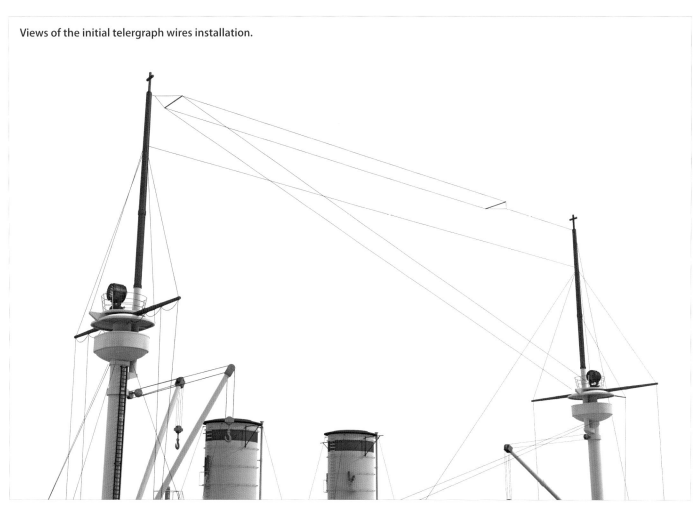

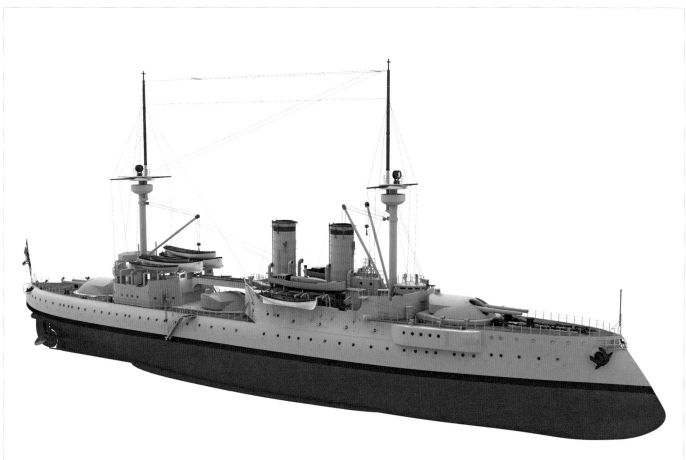

Overall view of the ship.

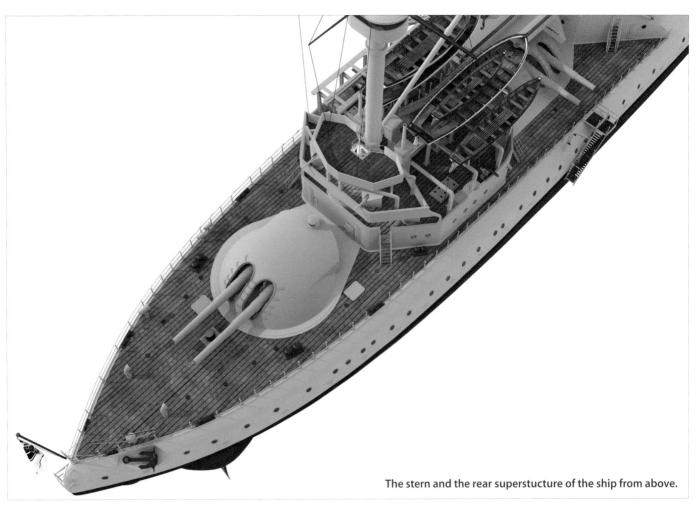

The stern and the rear superstucture of the ship from above.

The bow and the front superstucture of
the ship from above.

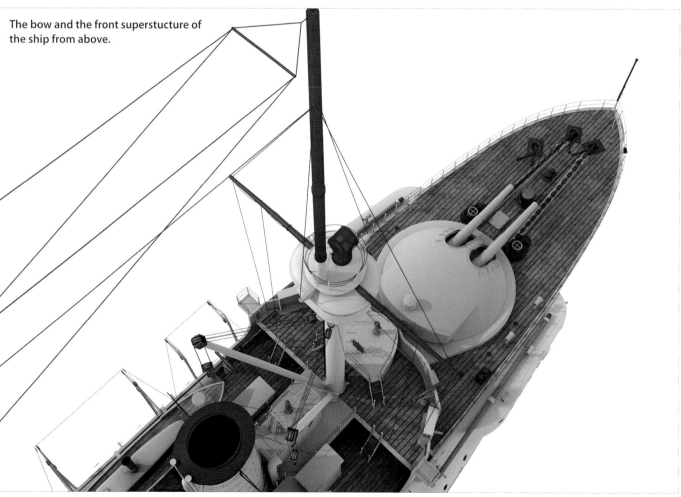

Bird-eye view of the ship.

Overall view of the ships bow.

# Inside you will find:

INTERESTING ARTICLES

ARCHIVAL PHOTOS

DRAWINGS

3D ILLUSTRATIONS
AND DRAWINGS OF
THE FAMOUS WARSHIPS

ANAGLYPH 3D

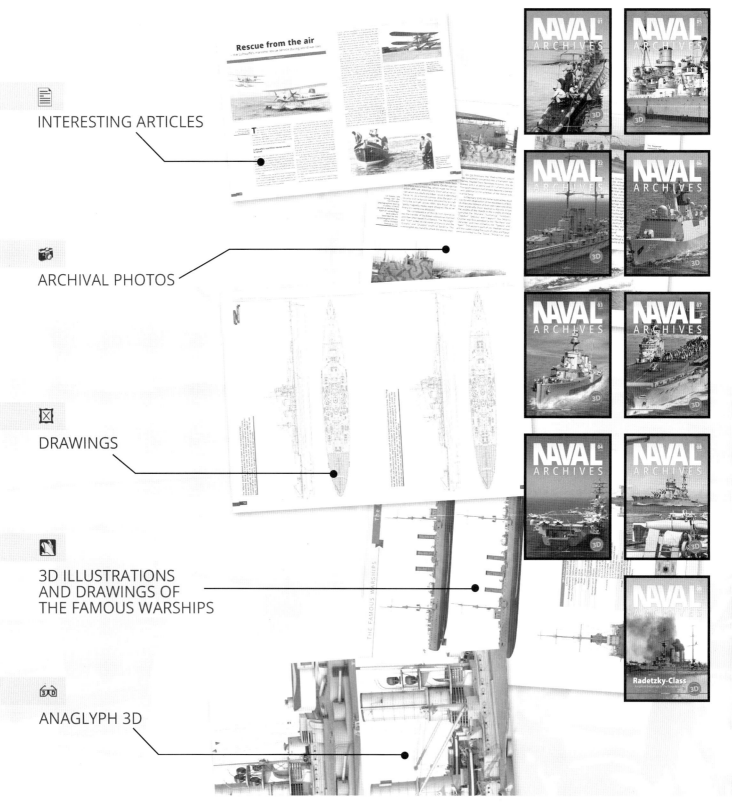

Visit our shop online **shop.kagero.pl**

**The Brandenburg-class Battleships 1890–1918** – Tassos Katsikas
LUBLIN 2019 • ISBN 978-83-66148-46-8
© All rights reserved. With the exception of quoting brief passages for the purposes of review, no part of this publication may be reproduced without prior written permission from the Publisher.
3D illustrations and captions, text: **Tassos Katsikas** • Design: **KAGERO STUDIO** – Łukasz Maj
**KAGERO Publishing** • www.kagero.pl, e-mail: kagero@kagero.pl, marketing@kagero.pl
Editorial office, Marketing, Distribution: **KAGERO Publishing**, Akacjowa 100, os. Borek, Turka, 20-258 Lublin 62, Poland, phone/fax (+48) 81 501 21 05
**w w w . k a g e r o . e u**

3D visualisations are based on the available photographs, drawings and other archive data, and should be treated only as author's attempt to recreate the original look of the particular machine as faithfully as possible. If you are in possession of materials to which author did not reach, and you would like to help us to develop a better publication, please contact the Publisher on: redakcja@kagero.pl